Barbie™

Barbie™ *Barbie*™

COOL COLORING

These besties love to pose for photos!
Color in this picture using the color chart as a guide.

STARLIGHT SEARCH

Brooklyn and Malibu were born to perform! Follow the lines that spell the word **SING** to help the girls find their way to the theater. You can travel up, down, left, and right.

START

I	S	C	L	S	N	G	S
B	I	N	A	R	G	B	E
S	P	G	T	Y	I	A	I
E	I	S	R	N	E	R	B
T	N	X	F	W	S	P	N
B	G	S	I	N	G	S	G
F	H	L	B	L	J	I	K
Q	U	H	P	T	F	N	G

FINISH

MUSICAL MUDDLE

Barbie's in a bit of a tangle! Follow the guitar leads to find out if she's plugged in and ready to rock!

A
B
C
D

ANIMAL ANTICS

The Central Park Zoo is one of Brooklyn's favorite places to visit. She loves learning about wildlife! Can you find five differences between these two scenes?

SECRET STAR

From rocking out with her BFF to dancing gracefully,
Barbie can do anything! Can you circle the matching silhouette?

FASHION FIX

Rafa creates costumes for Malibu and Brooklyn's performances!
He dreams of seeing his designs on the big stage one day.
List all the words you can make using the letters in:

COSTUME DESIGNER

DOUBLE DIVAS

Strike a pose! Which of these pictures are the same?
Color in the matching pair!

SIDEWALK SNACKS

The Big City is full of street vendors selling lots of different foods!
Can you find all the tasty treats in this puzzle using the word
bank below? Some letters have been added to help you.

PRETZEL
VEGGIE BURGER
PITA

FALAFEL
SALAD
GYRO
PIZZA

HOT DOG
PEANUTS
CHURROS

CUSTOM COLOR

For Brooklyn and Malibu, the sidewalk is their runway as they strut in their cosmic outfits! Color in their dresses with lots of bright colors.

STREET SALE

Brooklyn shops at local street markets to support
small businesses! Malibu wants to go bargain hunting at this one.
See if you can spot all eight items hidden in this scene.

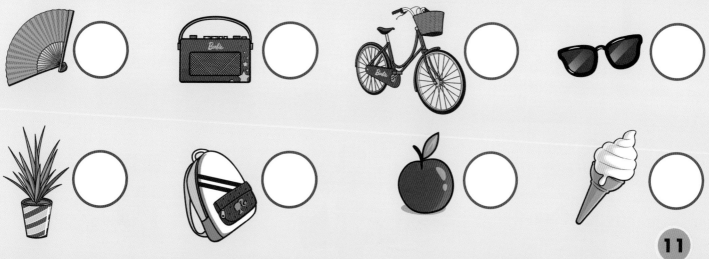

JIGSAW JUMBLE

Brooklyn and Malibu make their rockstar dreams
come true in the city that never sleeps!
Select the pieces that complete this musical puzzle.

RAINDROP DOTS

Compared to the sunny West, there's a lot more rain on the East Coast! Starting at number one, connect the dots to reveal how Barbie is sheltering from the storm, then color in this picture.

COSTUME CREATOR

Help Rafa design a fabulous dress for the show!
Decorate this one with different patterns and colors
using your brightest pencils or crayons.

MUSICAL MYSTERY

What is Brooklyn's favorite instrument?
Cross out the letters that appear twice in this grid to find out!

C	N	G	P	O	V	J	M
B	S	Y	D	U	F	H	L
I	K	Q	J	W	X	Z	S
W	X	O	D	Q	C	N	T
L	M	H	A	Y	V	P	Z
	K	F	B	R			

The word is:

_____

SKYLINE STICKERS

Use your stickers to bring this city scene to life!

16

BROADWAY BESTIES

Are you and your bestie like Brooklyn and Malibu?
Take this quiz to find out!

QUESTION	OPTION A	OPTION B
Does your BFF love . . .	☐ Dancing	☐ Singing
Fave food	☐ Fruit Salad	☐ Caesar Salad
Fave animal	☐ Dog	☐ Cat
Does your BFF prefer . . .	☐ Fall	☐ Summer
Fave hobby	☐ Roller skating	☐ Cycling
Ideal spotlight solo	☐ Playing guitar	☐ Ballet

What's Your Bestie Rating?

How many matching answers do you have?

0-3 You may not always be in sync, but you'll always be there for each other.

4-6 You two have got each other's back! Best friends for life!

SPOTLIGHT SEARCH

It's time to shine! Can you find all the words listed below?
Don't forget to look across, down, backwards, and diagonally!

CAST	COSTUME	LIGHTING	SHOW
CHORUS	CURTAIN	MAKEUP	SING
CONCERT	DANCE	MUSICAL	STAGE

S	M	C	U	R	T	A	I	N	B
L	D	O	A	H	Q	U	H	P	F
C	E	M	U	T	S	O	C	T	M
A	F	A	S	D	B	S	Y	K	U
S	L	K	H	A	I	Q	Z	T	S
T	R	E	C	N	O	C	S	U	I
H	I	U	G	C	R	U	H	J	C
O	D	P	W	E	R	Q	O	K	A
B	V	S	K	O	D	Y	W	P	L
L	I	G	H	T	I	N	G	D	A
H	F	C	T	U	E	G	A	T	S

DESIGNER DRAWING

These girls love to accessorize! Malibu spotted this bag at a cute boutique uptown. Can you draw another one for Brooklyn? Using the grid as your guide, copy the picture square by square. Don't forget to decorate it!

DELI DILEMMA

Brooklyn shows Malibu the best delis in the city. There's so much food, but not enough time to eat it all! Complete the image using the pieces below, then work out which goes where and write the letter of each piece in the correct spaces.

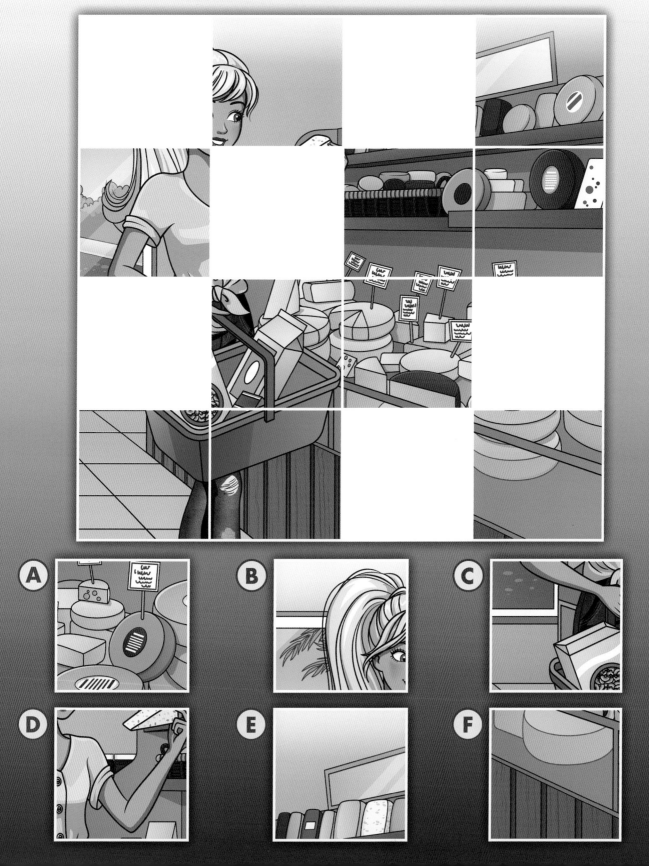

A

B

C

D

E

F

MYSTERY MESSAGE

Cross out the word CITY every time you see it. When you see a letter that is not part of the word, write it in the stars below to find a message from Malibu to Brooklyn. The first CITY has been done for you.

~~CITY~~ CITYACITY
NCITYYCITYTCI
TYHCITYICITYN
CITYGCITYICIT
YSCITYPCITYOC
ITYSCITYSCITY
ICITYBCITYLCI
TYCITYECITY

PUZZLING PUPPY

Gato has been chasing a ball through Central Park—now he's lost! Help the girls navigate the maze to find Rafa's pup.

START

FINISH

PICTURE PERFECT

Which of these pairs of fashionistas is different from the rest?
Circle the odd one out.

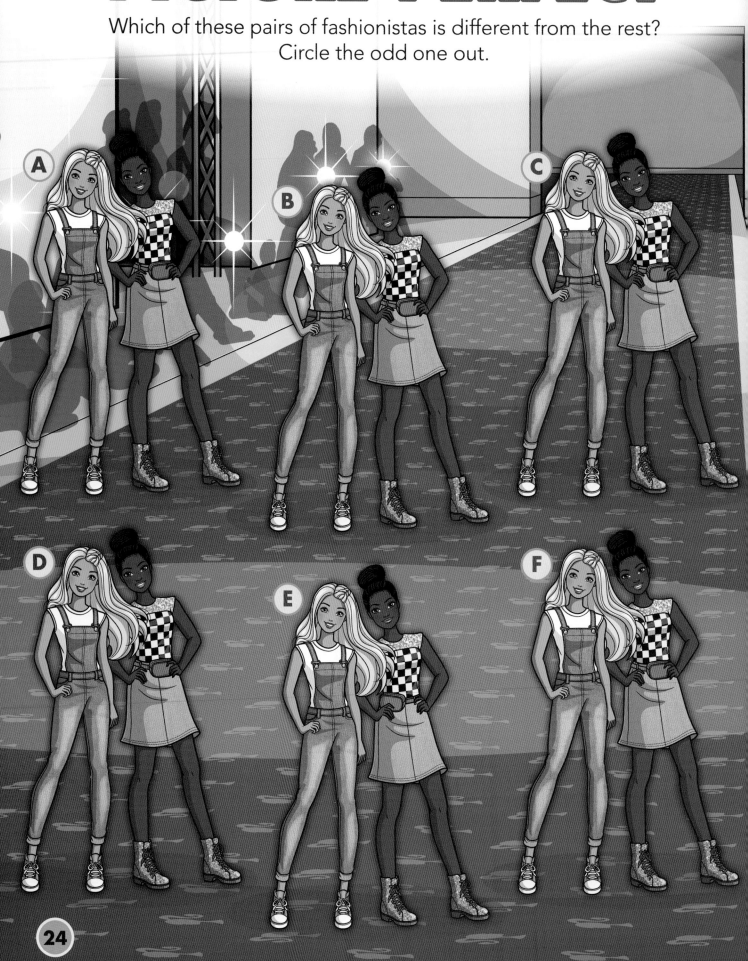

TREASURE HUNT

Barbie and her friends enjoy challenging themselves with puzzles, like this treasure hunt! Help them find all the items by writing down each coordinate below! One has been done for you.

STAY ON TRACK

Brooklyn and Malibu need to use the subway to travel across the city!
Help them by changing the word **RAIL** to **BAND**, one letter at a time,
to make a new word without rearranging the letters.
Example: **LATE** to **LANE**

RAIL

A way to travel by boat.

Past tense of "say."

Put down gently.

Earth surface not covered by water.

BAND

TIME TO SHINE!

The girls want to make their next performance even better than the last. Practice makes perfect! How many times can you find the word **SHINE** in this grid? Write your answer in the box below.

CREATE YOUR OWN CITYSCAPE

Doodle your own city skyline!

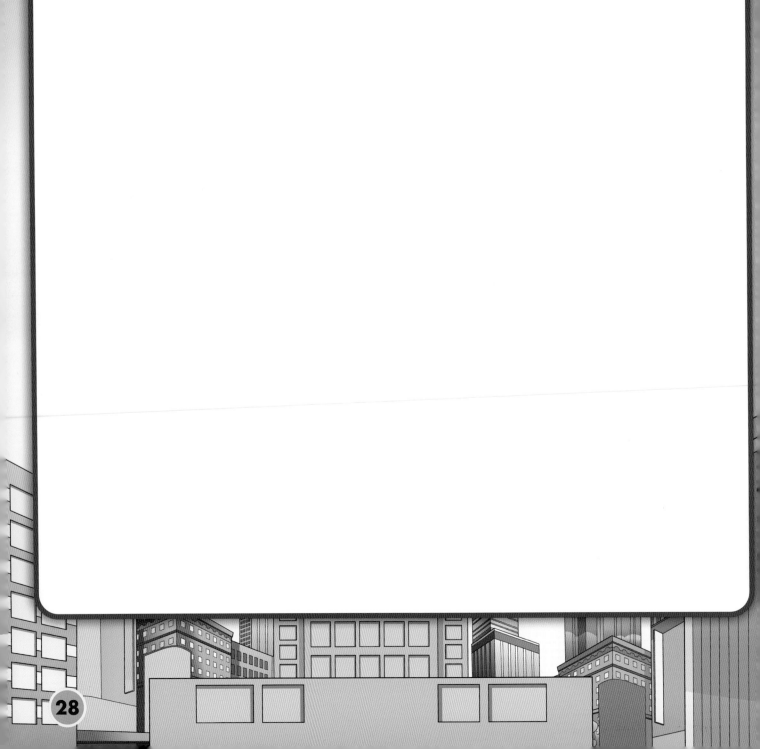

STICKER SEQUENCE

Using your stickers, complete the pattern by filling in the empty square in each row.

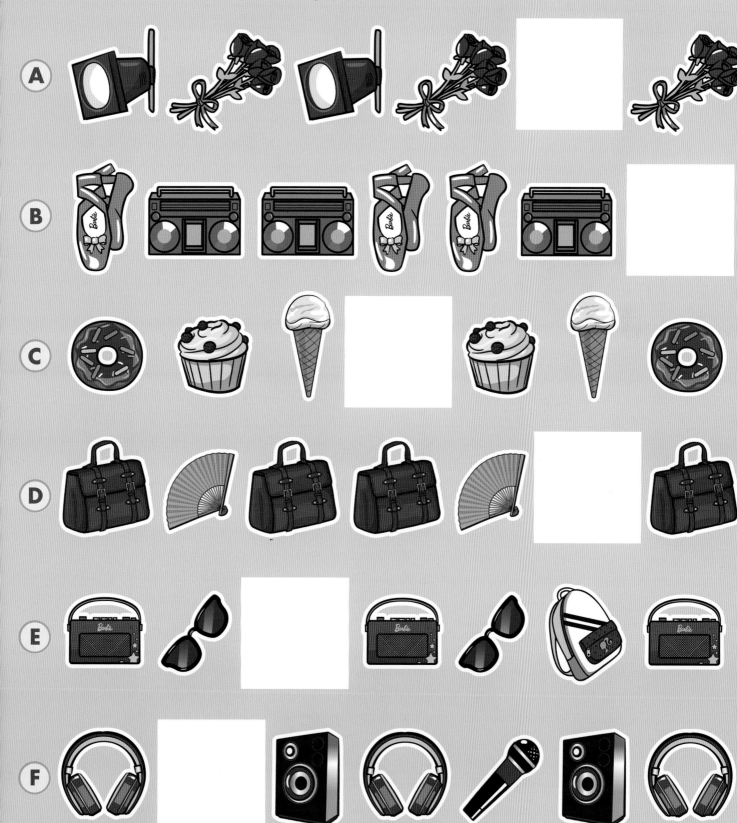

IT'S SHOWTIME!

Find out which instrument the girls are going to play at the Spotlight performance! Write your answer below.

1. Move 2 spaces right   2. Move 3 spaces down
3. Move 2 spaces right   4. Move 3 spaces up

Brooklyn and Malibu are playing the

_____!

ANSWERS

PAGE 3 - STARLIGHT SEARCH

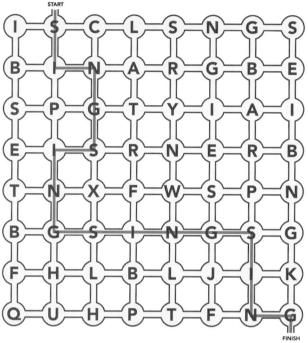

PAGE 4 - MUSICAL MUDDLE
A is plugged in.

PAGE 5 - ANIMAL ANTICS

PAGE 6 - SECRET STAR
D is the matching silhouette.

PAGE 8 - DOUBLE DIVAS
A and E are the same.

PAGE 9 - SIDEWALK SNACKS

PAGE 11 - STREET SALE

PAGE 12 - JIGSAW JUMBLE

PAGE 15 - MUSICAL MYSTERY
The word is: GUITAR

31

PAGE 19 - SPOTLIGHT SEARCH

S	M	C	U	R	T	A	I	N	B
L	D	O	A	H	Q	U	H	P	F
C	E	M	U	T	S	O	C	T	M
A	F	A	S	D	B	S	Y	K	U
S	L	K	H	A	I	Q	Z	T	S
T	R	E	C	N	O	C	S	U	I
H	I	U	G	C	R	U	H	J	C
O	D	P	W	E	R	Q	O	K	A
B	V	S	K	O	D	Y	W	P	L
L	I	G	H	T	I	N	G	D	A
H	F	C	T	U	E	G	A	T	S

PAGE 21 - DELI DILEMMA

PAGE 22 - MYSTERY MESSAGE

ANYTHING IS POSSIBLE!

PAGE 23 - PUZZLING PUPPY

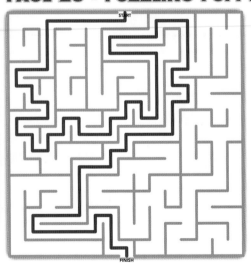

PAGE 24 - PICTURE PERFECT

E is different from the rest.

PAGE 25 - TREASURE TRAIL

 B 2
 E 1
 G 3
 A 4
 E 5
 C 6

PAGE 26 - STAY ON TRACK

RAIL - SAIL - SAID - LAID - LAND - **BAND**

PAGE 27 - TIME TO SHINE!

The word **SHINE** appears 20 times in this grid.

PAGE 29 - STICKER SEQUENCE

(A)

(B)

(C)

(D)

(E)

(F)

PAGE 30 - IT'S SHOWTIME!

Brooklyn and Malibu are playing the GUITAR!